CELEBRATING THE CITY OF HERAKLION

Celebrating the City of Heraklion

Walter the Educator

Silent King Books

Copyright © 2024 by Walter the Educator

All rights reserved. No part of this book may be reproduced in any manner whatsoever without written permission except in the case of brief quotations embodied in critical articles and reviews.

First Printing, 2024

Disclaimer

This book is a literary work; the story is not about specific persons, locations, situations, and/or circumstances unless mentioned in a historical context. Any resemblance to real persons, locations, situations, and/or circumstances is coincidental. This book is for entertainment and informational purposes only. The author and publisher offer this information without warranties expressed or implied. No matter the grounds, neither the author nor the publisher will be accountable for any losses, injuries, or other damages caused by the reader's use of this book. The use of this book acknowledges an understanding and acceptance of this disclaimer.

Celebrating the City of Heraklion is a little collectible souvenir book that belongs to the Celebrating Cities Book Series by Walter the Educator. Collect them all and more books at WaltertheEducator.com

USE THE EXTRA SPACE TO TAKE NOTES AND DOCUMENT YOUR MEMORIES

HERAKLION

IN THE HEART OF CRETE, WHERE LEGENDS WHISPER LOUD,

Celebrating the City of Heraklion

Lies Heraklion, where history is endowed.

A city veiled in myths, with labyrinthine streets,

Where tales of gods and kings the old stone walls repeat.

Beneath the azure sky, where olive branches sway,

Heraklion stands proud, where past and present play.

Amidst the ruins of Knossos, echoes of a throne,

A minotaur's labyrinth, tales of heroes known.

Yet beyond the ancient, a modern city thrives,

Celebrating the City of
Heraklion

Where bougainvillea blooms and the Aegean breeze arrives.

Through Venetian arches and Ottoman gates,

The pulse of Heraklion, where culture resonates.

In the morning's first light, fishermen cast their nets,

As the city awakens, with whispers the sun sets.

Mornings at the kafenio, with strong Greek coffee,

Evenings in the tavernas, where laughter flows free.

Wander through the market, where spices perfume the air,

Hear the vendors' stories, with a zest beyond compare.

In the warmth of Cretan sun, where hearts are bold and kind,

Heraklion beckons, to all who seek and find.

Celebrating the City of Heraklion

Olive groves surround, on hills where history stands,

From ancient Minoans' legacy to artists' hands.

Through the narrow alleys, where time slows its pace,

Feel the spirit of Heraklion, a timeless embrace.

In the maze of streets, where voices blend and fade,

Whispers of poets and painters, where dreams are made.

Underneath the starlit sky, tales of love and woe,

Heraklion's essence, in every ebb and flow.

The fortress of Koules, guarding harbors and dreams,

Where waves of centuries crash, in rhythmic streams.

From Byzantine churches to mosques' solemn call,

Heraklion's mosaic, where diverse cultures enthrall.

On summer evenings, as music fills the air,

In tavernas and squares, hearts gather and share.

A symphony of tongues, in stories old and new,

Heraklion's narrative, in every shade and hue.

Seasons drift like shadows, in olive-scented breeze,

From the heights of Mount Juktas to the Cretan seas.

In the pulse of Heraklion, where time finds its peace,

Past and present mingle, in rhythms that won't cease.

Celebrating the City of
Heraklion

ABOUT THE CREATOR

Walter the Educator is one of the pseudonyms for Walter Anderson. Formally educated in Chemistry, Business, and Education, he is an educator, an author, a diverse entrepreneur, and he is the son of a disabled war veteran. "Walter the Educator" shares his time between educating and creating. He holds interests and owns several creative projects that entertain, enlighten, enhance, and educate, hoping to inspire and motivate you. Follow, find new works, and stay up to date with Walter the Educator™

at WaltertheEducator.com

www.ingramcontent.com/pod-product-compliance
Lightning Source LLC
LaVergne TN
LVHW012050070526
838201LV00082B/3897